200 Reasons I Love You

Author Anonymous

PublishAmerica
Baltimore

ISBN: 1-4137-4566-0
PUBLISHED BY PUBLISHAMERICA, LLLP
www.publishamerica.com
Baltimore

Printed in the United States of America

Acknowledgments

I would like to thank my wife for her love, my father for teaching me how to be a man, and my mother for teaching me what to look for in a woman. I would also like to thank Alan Strickland and Craig Butterworth for their contributions to my life. Most of all, I thank God for his many blessings.

Foreword

I am writing this book for several reasons. First, I want my wife to know that I really love her and am very thankful for her. Second, I don't believe I could ever adequately speak the words I have written in this book to her. And third, I want her to have this expression of my love for her for the rest of her life. I am writing anonymously because I want it to be a complete surprise to my wife. She does not know about the book and I will not tell her about it.

I do have some concerns. Doing something like this is very much out of character for me. I am not verbally expressive and I don't often (if ever) tell my wife the things I have written to her here. I don't think she would suspect that I would ever do something like this, and one of my concerns is that she never reads it because she thinks there is no possibility that I wrote it. I hope and believe that she eventually will read it, and when she does, I know by the time she puts it down she will know that this is written for her.

To My Wife

From the time I was a boy up until the time I got married, I prayed every night for the woman who would become my wife.

It started when I was 12 and I prayed for God to watch over you, help you through any difficulties, and prepare us for each other. I did not know you then, but I knew that you would someday become the most important person in my life, and that God would find someone who was my perfect mate.

He did.

Not only are you my perfect mate, you are infinitely more wonderful than anyone I could ever have imagined. That is why I have decided to do this – to take a little bit of time to write down a few of the reasons I love you. It will be easy to write the reasons I love you. The difficult part is knowing that when you read this, it will not be adequate to fully express the depth of my love for you.

No words can.

1

I love waking up with you. When I look over at your cute, groggy smile in the morning, my heart jumps.

2

I love the way you greet me in the morning. You seem so excited to start a new day together. Most days it seems like you are about to jump out of your skin with excitement. You greet me with an ecstatic, "Hello Sunshine!" while you bounce around and pepper me with kisses. How could I help but love you.

3

I love your smile in the morning, and how you hug me tight, then let me go and as I start to walk away to get ready for work, you pull me back with another ferocious hug. You look so cute in your pajamas, still waking up and so happy. And when I notice that your curling iron is plugged into my side of the sink again, you shrug your shoulders innocently and say, "I love you." You are too cute for me to be mad, so I just tell you that I love you too as I plug it in on your side.

4

I love the way we seem to become more and more like each other the longer we are married. I have seen myself change and become more like you in many ways over the past years, and I am grateful for it. I am much more organized and cleaner (especially my ears) than I used to be, thanks to you. It is also funny to see you taking on some of my traits. Sorry about that.

5

I love that you let me sleep in. I don't know if you are really quiet or if I can just sleep through anything (including the fire alarm one night), but in any case, thanks for not feeling like you need to wake me up when you get up.

6

I love your lists. I didn't realize how stressful my life was until I married you. I was trying to keep all these lists in my head of things to do and buy. You showed me that I could just write them down and forget about them. Now if I could only figure out a way to remember to bring the list with me to the store.

7

I love your attitude. When I feel down about myself, you always point out all the positives that I seem to be overlooking in my life. I would have to say your positive attitude is your best attribute. You always see sunshine in every situation. It makes people want to be around you and makes me love you more.

8

I love your body, especially the curvy parts.

9

I love dancing with you. I fell in love with you on the dance floor. You were so fun and durable and patient with me, and you obviously don't embarrass easily, or you wouldn't have married me after all the dancing we have done together.

10

I love going on walks with you. The time seems to fly when we are walking and talking, and we always seem closer to each other when we get back home. I also appreciate that you remind me to wear my "special" underwear so that my legs don't get chapped.

11

I love our midday phone calls. More often than not we are both too busy to talk much, but it is always nice to hear "I love you" during the middle of a workday.

12

I love calling you little pet names – "Sweetie Pie," "Pumpkin Pie," "Sweet Pea," "Sugar Dumpling," "Sugar Bear," "Honey Muffin," "Sunshine." Hey, most of these have to do with food. I wonder how that happened. By the way, some of my co-workers make fun of me for calling you by these names.

13

I love getting to run with you some mornings. After asking me for weeks, I finally caved in and got up early to jog. It is great talking to you about things going on in our lives and it makes the workout part so easy. I know my parents used to wake up very early in the morning to go on walks and it really meant a lot to them, especially my mom. Now I see why.

14

I love looking at old pictures of you. You were so cute in sixth grade with your feathered hair. If someone would have pointed you out to me back then and said that you were the girl I was going to end up marrying, I would have been very excited.

15

I love your cooking. On those special occasions when you decide to cook, it is usually something sweet and it turns out delicious. And you know how much food means to me.

16

I love your tender lips. While I also think you have really nice shoulders, those shoulders have never kissed me.

17

I love kissing you hello.

18

I love kissing you goodbye.

19

I love kissing you in between hello and goodbye.

20

I love the transformation you make when you are hungry and/or tired. It is hilarious and so predictable. You get feisty and irritable and easily annoyed (but not angry) and that is when you are really fun to pick on and play with.

21

I love that you know exactly what I am thinking when no one else has a clue. You read me like an open book when others have no idea what is going on inside my head. They don't know how simple I am.

22

I love that you point out my bad habits and try to help me improve. Actually, I usually don't like it at the time, but appreciate it later (kind of like a flu shot). In so many ways you make me a much better person than I would be without you.

23

I love to laugh with you. Even though it is usually at my expense, it is wonderful to laugh and see you laugh. I can really tell that you love me when you laugh.

24

I love your dedication. You have accomplished so much because you are so dedicated to whatever you decide to do. I have seen it in your school, work, and extracurricular activities. You always rise to the top because you throw yourself fully into whatever you are working on.

25

I love that you pop my back when I am feeling like it is a little out of line.

26

I love that your family is so important to you. My dad always told me that when picking out a wife I should look at the girl's mom, because that is likely how she would turn out. Dad was right. I think both our moms are great, and I see that you have taken on some of your mom's excellent attributes.

27

I love that my family likes you so much and that you get along with them.

28

I love that you clean out my car every once in a while, just because.

29

I love that you met me in my physical prime. Although it doesn't seem to bother you, it is frustrating for me to look in the mirror and see the bigger belly, receding hairline and thick patch of hair on my back. By the way, thanks for shaving the back patch sometimes when we go swimming so that it doesn't look like a shark fin. This next time it grows back, it will probably be long enough to comb up over my head, hiding my bald spot.

30

I love that you tell me that you think I am getting cuter all the time, even though we both know the truth.

31

I love that you pray for me. As you know, I need it.

32

I love that you "help me drive.". Even though I sometimes seem annoyed by your overreaction to traffic situations, I know that you have saved us from multiple wrecks when I did not see something that you did. There, now you have it in writing.

33

I love the way you hold babies. It is a beautiful thing to see and it has always seemed perfectly natural to you. I also like how you pass them off to me right when they start to get fussy so that when they start to really scream everyone sees that I am the one holding them.

34

I love riding in the car with you in the morning. You are so cute as you stare off into space, kind of still waking up. You aren't much for talking a lot of times, but we sit with each other listening to the radio and enjoying each other's company.

35

I love your work ethic and admire the way you work hard at whatever you do.

36

I love that you have loosened up a lot since we first got married. You used to be a lot more intense in some areas, and now you are so easy-going.

37

I love that a kiss on the cheek gets me a smile from you every time. It's a great deal.

38

I love reading the Bible with you at night. I can't believe how much ground we cover, just reading a little bit each night.

39

I love praying with you in the morning. Having the opportunity to speak with God is awesome enough, but sharing that with you makes it incredible. I have also noticed that it is very difficult to keep problems between us unresolved for more than a day, because neither of us wants to pray until we work out our issue.

40

I love talking with you on road trips. We have some of the best conversations about life and what is important on our trips, and there is something calming about driving in the car with you. It really relaxes me and draws me close to you.

41

I love when you accidentally mix up old sayings and combine parts of different ones together. For example, "crack me up" + "freak me out" turns into "crack me out." Or "sharp as a tack" + "smart as a whip" becomes "smart as a tack." It is almost like a game for me to try to figure out which two you are combining together and we always have a good laugh once I figure it out.

42

I love kissing you at red lights when we are driving somewhere. It seems like we do this more and more the longer we are married. I think it is a good tradition.

43

I love getting emails from you throughout the day. It is really nice to hear a little bit about how your day is going.

44

I love going to lunch with you. I love food. I love you. It is a great combination.

45

I love watching football on TV with your dad and grandpa.

46

I love the fact that you go to buffets with me even though I'm not the greatest conversationalist when I'm in the vicinity of that much food. It happens every time. I get that far-away look in my eyes as I focus on the task of eating as much as I can to get my money's worth. I know that it probably isn't too pleasurable for you to see me "In the Zone," but you go with me anyway and I appreciate you letting me share that experience with you.

47

I love that I can talk to you about my fears without even the thought that it might change how you feel about me if you see my vulnerabilities.

48

I love falling asleep in your arms, even though what usually happens is that I start jumping around because I'm having an action-packed dream and you have to give me the old elbow nudge to the abdomen to get me the heck off you. Of course I never remember the elbow nudge the next morning because I was half asleep when it happened, but you're always there to remind me.

49

I love jogging with you on Saturdays because we usually aren't rushed, and we get to go exploring outside together.

50

I love getting your advice. Nine times out of ten you give me good advice, and you always are able to see things from a different and usually better perspective.

51

I love that you are so easily pleased (hey you must be if you married me). You definitely cannot be considered High Maintenance because I know if I keep you fed and watered, you are usually happy and have a good attitude.

52

I love hearing about your unusual childhood pets. Who else's favorite pet growing up was a turtle? Who else had hermit crabs, frogs and one-winged birds as pets?

53

I love hearing stories about your childhood pets over and over and over again. Like the one about you building a fort for your turtle, or the one about you taping a piece of string to his back to make a leash and taking him on walks outside. I bet those were some long walks.

54

I love that you listen to my childhood stories over and over again, especially the ones about playing in the bayou.

55

I love that I can call you during the day and ask you to pray for me, and you stop what you are doing and pray. I did this today and you prayed and God answered. What a great blessing it is to have you.

56

I love the thought of growing old with you. I see older couples holding hands, and I know we are going to be all shriveled and cute and still in love some day.

57

I love that we can have a conversation without even saying a word. Just a look, a facial expression, or the way you hold your arms tells me what is on your mind. It is like we read each other's thoughts sometimes.

58

I love that you are so modest about your accomplishments. Ever since we first started dating and you were too embarrassed to tell me you got baseball tickets for making straight A's, you have never even shown a hint of bragging about what you have accomplished.

59

I love holding your hand in movies where it is dark.

60

I love that you seem to believe that if you eat food from my plate, somehow the calories from that food don't count against you. I guess they magically disappear if it is not food that you ordered. That is why I always end up getting enough for both of us.

61

I love that you break cookies and pretzels apart because everybody knows a little broken piece of cookie or pretzel doesn't have as many calories as a whole cookie or pretzel (even if you eat all the pieces?).

62

I love driving you home at night. Sometimes you want to talk about your day. Sometimes you want to hear about my day. Sometimes you want to vent your frustrations. And sometimes we just ride in silence, but it is always nice because if I have to drive home anyway, I might as well be with you.

63

I love telling you how beautiful you look in the morning. You really do look beautiful, and especially in the morning after you get ready for work. I always think, "WOW, THAT'S MY WIFE!"

64

I love hearing you kick the scale into the wall in the morning when it gives you an answer you don't like, and then mutter under your breath, "Stupid scale." I agree. It is a stupid scale!

65

I love that you call me Sunshine. It probably wouldn't be a big deal to me. You call me a lot of things, but I know how much you really like sunny days and really dislike overcast days, so you calling me Sunshine means a lot.

66

I love traveling with you and seeing new places. Even places neither of us would like if we went to them separately seem pretty neat when we go together.

67

I love napping with you on Sunday afternoons. I don't know what it is about Sundays, but it is just nice to lie down and take a nice long nap with you.

68

I love our little back and forth conversations that go something like…
Me: "Love you."
You: "Love you more."
Me: "Miss you already."
It has almost become a ritual, like us kissing at red lights or praying in the mornings together.

69

I love that you always want to spend time with me.

70

I love that you seem sad whenever we part company because you know you will miss me.

71

I love that sometimes you pretend to be all sad because I don't appreciate you, when what you are really doing is angling for another foot massage. You're so predictable sometimes.

72

I love that you are enjoying that new foot massage machine I just bought you. It makes my life so much easier.

73

I love toting you around places, because I know how much you like being toted. It reminds me of when I used to take our dogs for rides in the car. They were so excited to look out the window.

74

I love making you giant homemade birthday cards.

75

I love writing little love notes on sticky pads and hiding them for you around the house. Actually, it is really your reaction that I love a lot more than the writing or the hiding.

76

I love finding your earplugs all over our bedroom. It's like an Easter egg hunt every morning. It is especially funny when I roll out of bed and groggily wonder, "What's that sticking to my back?" How many ears do you have anyway?

77

I love that when you ask me if I want to try something on your plate at a restaurant, and I say, "Sure, just a little bite," that you give me a big piece of whatever it is you are eating.

78

I love that you usually smell pretty nice, except sometimes at weddings.

79

I love that you encourage me exactly when I need encouragement.

80

I love that you knock me back down to earth in a hurry when I am "too encouraged" with myself.

81

I love that you are just so darned fun to hang out with. We had a great time today just laughing and hanging out and acting crazy together.

82

I love that you want to spend all your time with me. Although I often wonder why, it makes me feel good to know that you enjoy my company.

83

I love that you know what I want or mean without me having to waste words. I am naturally quiet, so I really like our efficient nonverbal communication.

84

I love that you are so strong. Your strength of character is one of the things that hooked me on you.

85

I love your big sparkly eyes. They tell me so much.

86

I love snuggling with you in the morning, especially on cold winter mornings when it is dark outside and we are under the comforter. It does make for a difficult time getting out of bed.

87

I love when I finally do roll out of bed, coming into the kitchen in the morning and seeing you hunched over your box of Lucky Charms, half asleep and eating straight out of the box.

88

I love your hugsnuggliness.

89

I love that you look like the woman I wanted to marry when I grew up. When I was a kid, I had an idea of what I wanted my wife to look like and you fit the image.

90

I love the fact that you breathe so heavily when you fall into a deep sleep. I sometimes just lie there and listen to you, laughing inside.

91

I love that you rarely make me go shopping with you. You know how the mall just drains my energy, and it seems we are both happier when I don't go shopping with you.

92

I love that when I do go shopping with you, you don't have high expectations and it doesn't bother you if I just stand outside the stores and people-watch or entertain myself in some other way.

93

I love that you think the whole bed is "your side."

94

I love that a few of the people you have worked with really made you appreciate me.

95

I love that you are wise beyond your years, yet still silly and playful.

96

I love that you have a proper perspective. You know what is important, and you know what is not as important, and you live your life accordingly. I guess this also relates back to you being wise beyond your years.

97

I love that you and I get better and better at kissing the longer we are married. I guess that thing they say about practice is true.

98

I love your mental toughness. You deal with some real characters in your daily life and you handle them well. You also handle family crises like a champ. They bring out qualities in you that I didn't know you had.

99

I love your consistency. When you commit to something or set a goal, you really stay dedicated until you accomplish what you have set out to do.

100

I love your patience. You need it living with me.

101

I love hearing about your crazy dreams. It is fun while pulling your earplugs off my back in the morning to hear the strange tales your mind concocted to keep you entertained while you were asleep the night before.

102

I love that while you don't always sleep well when I'm next to you (from me tossing and turning), you definitely don't sleep well when I'm away. It makes me feel like I am contributing.

103

I love that I get to call you "Sweetness" – the coolest part (and I doubt you know this) is that I borrowed the nickname from a football player, Walter Payton. Like you, he was one of the greatest of all time.

104

I love that you can laugh at yourself. Some of our biggest laughs are about things that we have done.

105

I love that you get crazier and crazier the longer we are married, and the fact that you blame me for it.

106

I love that you don't stress about small things – or usually big things for that matter.

107

I love that you don't mind when sometimes in the morning I make bird noises.

108

I love holding you when you are sad.

109

I love that you will usually write the cards or letters from us since my handwriting looks like a 3rd grader's.

110

I love watching you teach Sunday school. You handle yourself so well and you have great wisdom and insight.

111

I love sharing a hymnal with you at church. It gives us an excuse to stand closer together.

112

I love that you have now learned to tolerate a lot of things that used to bother you about me. You have become a lot more accepting of my peculiarities, such as yelling at the TV when sports are on, or getting up at 3:00 a.m. to go fishing (well, maybe someday you won't mind the early morning fishing trips).

113

I love that you don't tolerate everything from me. You force me to better myself, which in the long run helps make me a better person than I would be otherwise.

114

I love that you are level-headed when I sometimes am not (see "when sports are on TV" above).

115

I love trying new restaurants with you. It always seems like a first date when we go someplace new.

116

I love that you laugh when I talk about getting a walk-in freezer to store meat, even though you know I am serious. Just think about it. We could have a whole side dedicated to your ice cream sandwiches.

117

I love that you care so much for your family.

118

I love surprising you on Valentines Day with a giant crazy card.

119

I love that you feel all sorry for yourself when you get tired and then a few days later when I am still giving you a hard time about it, you can laugh.

120

I love driving the old folks to church with you and breaking down the previous night's football game with an 88-year-old lady who loves the team as much as I do.

121

I love that you prayed for wisdom in the hope that God would just supernaturally zap you with it, only to find that He chose to answer your prayer by putting you in a situation that would make you wise.

122

I love that your New Year's resolution for us was "More Kissin."

123

I love riding in elevators with you, especially alone where we can work on our New Year's resolution.

124

I love coming home to you from a weekend with the guys.

125

I love that for some reason, you don't believe you can get into bed until after I am already there. It is the funniest thing to see you completely exhausted at night, wanting to go to sleep, begging me to go to bed, yet still finding little things to do to keep you occupied until I actually get into bed. Then you immediately join me. Sometimes I purposely take a long time just to see if this will be the night you get into bed first.

126

I love working on the Sunday school lesson with you. We have such different styles of preparation and it is impressive to see all the research you do and to see how seriously you take it.

127

I love that when we are up there in front of the Sunday school class teaching the lesson and I look out at the sea of blank stares and half-asleep teenagers struggling to remain conscious after having their energy sapped by the previous night's activities, that I can look over and see you smiling at me.

128

I love praying for you.

129

I love watching TV with your granddad and seeing him slowly doze off. It is like watching two shows at once. His head starts nodding as he struggles to stay awake and pretty soon he is out like a light. I think it is because he can't hear the TV very well but doesn't want to say anything because he doesn't like his hearing aid. I wish I had a similar explanation for why the teenagers nod off during Sunday school.

130

I love what I have found to be a very nice part of our marriage – nude naps.

131

I love that the only gift you ever seem to ask for from me are "Trifectas" (combination hand, feet, and shoulder massages).

132

I love watching you groggily cringe and then roll back over to your side of the bed with your back to me when you happen to accidentally get into the direct line of my "dragon" breath in the morning.

133

I love that in church sometimes you will dig your shoulder into my arm until I (usually slowly) get the message that you want me to put my arm around you.

134

I love thinking about you when I'm fishing.

135

I love the way playing basketball makes me miss you terribly. I still do not know why.

136

I love that you are always trying to get me to look for gray hairs to pick (like you have that many). I think the real reason you do that is because you just like me playing with your hair. You always seem more relaxed after a session of gray hair hunting.

137

I love the way you make fun of my heavy walking. For the record, I know I'm not going to sneak up on anybody but I don't think I am that loud.

138

I love that you are so fascinated with rocks. Of all the beautiful sights we saw on vacation, it was hilarious to see you get all excited about some of the rocks that were there. I'm glad we didn't bring home all of the ones you liked. Our suitcase was heavy enough.

139

I love that you are still afraid of the "Closet Monster." Luckily he is harmless as long as the closet light is out, or as I have found, as long as you think the closet light is out.

140

I love that you are the answer to this chubby junior high kid's prayer. I remember looking at my soft pudgy physique in the mirror and thinking, "I better start praying if I ever want to have a wife. It is going to take God a LONG time to get a decent woman ready for me!"

141

I love that you smell like roasted turkey after you go tanning. It always makes me hungry.

142

I love you sweaty and out of breath, especially after being beaten in one-on-one basketball again. Sure, you kick my butt in tennis and swimming, but you will never take me in basketball.

143

I love that you help Mother Nature along when it comes to our plants. You got out there with your little paintbrush and helped pollinate the buds on our fruit tree when the bees just weren't getting the job done.

144

I love that most of the time you pay the bills, balance the checkbook and keep us on budget. I really appreciate you doing these tedious tasks.

145

I love that you are such a deal-hound. It is impressive to see you at work clipping and filing coupons and taking advantage of every deal you find. You must be every marketing executive's worst nightmare: a smart, organized, frugal shopper who uses every coupon she finds. I'm often amazed at your skill in arbitraging the unfortunate stores you frequent.

146

I love that when it comes to personal finances, you are a complete player. You have a really strong offensive game with your earning potential. You play great defense by helping us live well below our means (coupon queen). And you distribute the ball well by giving liberally of your time, talent and money to the church and others. You are a great teammate.

147

I love that no matter where you are in the house or what you are doing, you always seem to know when the popcorn that I am making is done so that you can come get some. It is also funny that you don't want to see how much butter I put on it. Trust me, you don't want to know.

148

I love that you saved yourself for me. What a fun wedding we had, and the wedding night was incredible. Thank you for giving me such a wonderful wedding gift.

149

I love that you are sooooooo sexcellent.

150

I love that your love for me runs a very distant second to your love for God.

151

I love that you are such a leader. When you see that something needs to get done, you take the lead and rally the right people to do it. I have seen you do this in your work, at home, and at church. Of course at home your trick is to "rally" me to get it done by adding it to my list.

152

I love that you enjoy the classier, more constructive and uplifting TV programs like *Oprah* and all the home design shows and are not as interested in some of the lower quality shows. You have said it is because you want to be careful about what goes into your mind.

153

I love the fact that you get confused and sad when you hear married people say that they love their spouse, but are not "in love" with them anymore as a reason for divorce. My dad always said that love is 90% commitment and 10% feelings. The feelings rise and fall, but loving someone is being committed to them throughout the emotional highs and lows. I'm very glad that you believe love is a choice. You have told me that you can choose to love (be committed to) someone regardless of how you feel about them at any given time. If you did not believe this, I'm quite sure it would cause major problems in our marriage because being married to me is not always the most emotionally fulfilling experience.

154

I love seeing how you comfort your friends who are going through divorce. It only takes one spouse being uncommitted to break up a marriage, and it seems like this is the case too often with our friends. One spouse is committed to working through the issues and the other chooses to leave. It is devastating for the committed spouse, but your comfort and companionship to your friends going through these difficult times is unconditional. I can really see God's love shining through in your life during these times.

155

I love meeting older couples with you who have been married 50 and 60 years and asking them what the secret to their successful marriage is. Some of the answers are funny, but there is usually a common theme. I remember one lady who had been married 63 years didn't even hesitate when we asked what the key to their successful marriage was. She looked us in the eye and said with a lot of emotion that the key was, "HARD WORK!" Another man proclaimed with a lot of pride that they both knew their place that HE WORE THE PANTS IN THE FAMILY! He then said sheepishly that the key to their long and successful marriage was that his wife told him which pants to put on. Finally, another man and woman said that the key was that the husband had to give himself 100% to his wife and the wife had to give herself 100% to her husband. They kept saying not 50-50 or 75-25, but each one has to give 100% to the other.

156

I love that a lot of times when you finish working out you lean in, sniff my shirt and then curl up your nose and say, "You kind of stink." Then you say that I need a shower. The first time you did this, I felt pretty self-conscious, thinking I really did smell bad, but I soon figured out what you were really up to.

157

I love that you enjoy your garden so much. I like going out there to see what changes you have made, moving plants and stones here and there. I also think it is great that you have decided to name some of your favorite plants.

158

I love that no matter what I do, the cost is always measured in kisses. If I have to work late you say, "It's going to cost you some kisses." If I go away with the guys for the weekend, more kisses. Even if I am doing something for you like picking up your prescription, somehow you decide that you need to charge me for that in extra kisses.

159

I love lying with you in a hammock. It is so relaxing and I always seem to fall asleep instantly, especially if we are near water.

160

I love that if I tell you we need to leave for somewhere 5 minutes before we actually need to leave, then we are almost always on time. It took me a while to figure this out and I had to experiment with different times. I tried 15 and 10 minutes, but five extra minutes is all you ever really need, and sometimes you don't even need that much. As I'm sure you would point out, the biggest factor in determining if we get somewhere on time is whether I know where I am going.

161

I love that you think the fat squirrels around the neighborhood are out to get you. I think your squirrel conspiracy theory is hilarious because it is so out of character for you. It is funny to watch the reaction on your face when we are walking or jogging and you see a big squirrel in the path minding its own business. If it doesn't run right away you seem to assume that it is after you or "attacking you" as you like to tell your friends. You squeal and jump behind me, which usually startles the poor animal and typically causes it to lumber off. From my perspective, it looks like the squirrel is just waiting to see if we have anything to feed it before it takes off. I think that is why it is mainly the fat ones that "attack" you. They have been trained to take food from people, like the big glazed doughnut you saw one struggling with the other day.

162

I love that you have such wonderful friends. Some you have been close to for over 20 years and some you have just recently met. Some are much older and some younger, but you seem to have befriended so many people of exceptionally high character. It is really neat to see your interaction with them and commitment to them and to see how you all support each other, especially through difficult times.

163

I love the fact that you seem to really like it when I end letters or emails with the phrase, "Most Sincerely and Affectionately Yours." I got the phrase from a letter from the 1800s that we studied in English class in high school or college and thought it sounded nice, but I did not anticipate how much you would like it.

164

I love that even though most of your friends (especially the ones who got married later in life) have much nicer and more expensive wedding rings than you, it does not seem to bother you. I know I am always embarrassed to see the huge diamonds some of them are forced to lug around on their poor little fingers, but you have never let me think that the quality of the ring I put on your finger so many years ago when I was a man of considerably lesser means is important to you, even when I ask. I think this fact highlights your quality as a person who does not define herself by what she wears.

165

I love the way you dress. You always wear something tasteful, attractive and stylish for work or when we go out. You are a truly beautiful woman and the way you dress accentuates your natural elegance.

166

I love and am also continually surprised that you find such great deals on high quality, stylish outfits. I probably should be used to it by now, since you seem to find these deals all the time. But I am just starting to figure out how your network of shopping friends operates, looking out for deals and notifying the others when they see good ones. It is a pretty effective way to shop.

167

I love your hair falling down on my face, brushing and tickling my cheeks and blocking out everything in the room but your cute smile.

168

I love that you set aside articles that you think I will be interested in so that I can read them. It makes me realize that you are thinking about me.

169

I love that you peck away at the cookie dough when I am making a batch of my world famous walnut/chocolate chip/M&M cookies. It reminds me of a bird pecking away at seeds on the ground. Thanks for always being willing to test the quality of the dough before I put a batch in the oven. It is a tough job but someone has to do it.

170

I love that when we are on vacation together people will sometimes ask if we are on our honeymoon. We must look like we are in love.

171

I love the way you pack for a trip. You're an animal. There is no way you are going to leave anything behind that you might possibly need. If it is a weekend trip, you pack enough clothes for a week. Plus tennis rackets, golf clubs, bikes, every kind of over-the-counter and prescription medicine we have, etc. It is a good thing we have large suitcases, because you use them. I always think it is funny when we show up places with our car packed to the ceiling with stuff and see how little other people bring.

172

I love that you are always asking me to remind you to do something or write something down when we get home. I rarely remember to, but at least it shows that you still have confidence in my memory after all these years together.

173

I love that you have somehow adjusted to sleeping in the same bed with me. Early on it was a challenge. I give off enough thermal energy to power a small town. Over time you have learned to live with my nocturnal heat generation to the point that you now need several comforters to replace me if I am away on a trip.

174

I love the fact that you are addicted to snow cones. If you must have a vice, I guess snow cones are not so bad. I didn't realize how serious the addiction was when we first got married, but your history should have given me a clue. Your favorite childhood toy was a Snoopy snow cone maker. One of your best friends coincidentally worked at a snow cone stand in high school that you visited often. All the signs were there. When we started driving all over town looking for snow cone stands, I knew the problem was serious. I think one of the best investments I ever made was the industrial strength snow cone machine I bought you for your birthday. It wasn't cheap, but it paid for itself many times over just in the first few years.

175

I love that you know me so well and still love me anyway.

176

I love that you polish my work shoes for me when they start to get scraggly. You always make them look so nice and I really appreciate it. Of course you always charge me for the service…in kisses.

177

I love that you think about me when picking out your lip gloss. This may be some sort of defense mechanism stemming from the time you tried to pick one out that I didn't like and I told you that you could just kiss yourself with that one. On later reflection, maybe I could have worded that a bit more diplomatically (and not so loudly). By the way, I really like the raspberry and vanilla.

178

I love that a lot of times our thinking and desires seem to be completely in sync. Like the other day we were on a bike ride and you asked me what I wanted for dinner. You told me what you were thinking and it was the exact same thing, and somehow you knew before you said it that it was what I was thinking. It was amazing. We seem to grow more alike the longer we are married. I just hope you don't start to look like me, too.

179

I love that you keep track of our appointments. You have a very nice system for keeping us organized and I really appreciate the effort you make to keep all of our commitments documented so that nothing falls through the cracks.

180

I love that when we go shopping for clothes for me, you are so efficient. You know I'm not there for the experience. I'm there to get what I need as quickly as possible and get the heck out. Because you know how I don't like to shop for clothes, you always find what I am looking for quickly and efficiently and I really appreciate that.

181

I love shopping for groceries with you. Wandering through a store full of food is always a fantastic experience, especially with the one I love.

182

I love the way you sort of hop when you walk when you are happy. It reminds me of a puppy who is excited to see its owner.

183

I love the way you sometimes "help" me up the stairs. When you put both hands on my fanny and push, I feel like I am as light as a feather floating up the staircase. Although sometimes I think you just do it because you like grabbing my behind.

184

I love that you are not concerned about what other people think of you. This is a quality that drew me to you in the beginning. You are confident in who you are as a person. You are independent in your thinking, open to new ideas and always searching for wisdom. You have values you live by that you are not willing to compromise. Basically, you are a woman of strong character. What a rare and priceless gift it is to be married to a woman like you.

185

I love that so far, each year of marriage with you seems better than the last.

186

I love that you often help me find little things that I am looking for when I lose them (keys, wallet, etc.). I have stopped asking you to help me find these things lately because you have seemed a little annoyed. You probably think I am not looking very hard before asking you because they always seem to be in plain sight. Instead of asking you, I have been asking God to help me find the little things and it turns out that he is really good at it, too.

187

I love your sandpapery-soft legs on days when you forget to shave them. They work great for back scratches.

188

I love that when I kiss you, you sometimes reply with a wispy, "I feel weak."

189

I love the way you look at me when I have a bag of potato chips tipped to the sky, my mouth around the bottom trying to get every last speck of salt and chip and grease to stick to my tongue. When I come up for air with chip pieces falling down around my chin and onto my shirt, you always seem to have a look of bewildered intrigue. It is the same look of disgusted fascination that I have seen on people's faces for years at the sight of me eating. I appreciate that this hasn't changed the way you feel about me.

190

I love that you voted me the winner of your "Sexiest Man Alive" award. Although it was close, I was able to edge out Brad Pitt again this year.

191

I love resting my head on and listening to your stomach. It sounds like the ocean.

192

I love the pictures of you as a toddler. You were built like a block, with your little arms, squatty legs, and rotund yet rock-solid belly. From the stories your relatives tell, you were fearless. You definitely were not "girly."

193

I love that you are so easy to shop for now. Probably because of the incredibly poor job I did picking out gifts for you early in our relationship (Elvis calendar, fishing rod that I later borrowed, etc.), you are all too willing to let me know exactly what you want now. This works best for everyone.

194

I love your ability to hang onto things, especially your clothes, for way past what most people would consider their normal useful life. This squirrel-esque tendency to store things for a long period of time just in case you need them later is probably the reason you still have socks with your high school mascot on them and definitely the reason your closet is five times larger than mine.

195

I love swimming with you.

196

I love locking foreheads with you for a close-up of your eyes.

197

I love dreaming with you about our future.

198

I love Eskimo kissing you.

199

I love how your leg shakes when you are happy or excited.

200

I love that when you pick this book up, you won't know who wrote it. But when you put it down, you will know it was written for you.

Printed in the United Kingdom
by Lightning Source UK Ltd.
108127UKS00003B/309